Survival

Could You Be A MOUSE ?

Photography – John Norris Wood
Illustrations – Derick Bown
Natural History and Expert Tips –
John Norris Wood

IDEALS CHILDREN'S BOOKS
Nashville, Tennessee

Each time you turn the page, you score *SURVIVAL* points.

If you turn to a page you have been to before, you don't score anything.

Count your moves. Every time you turn the page, that's one move. If two players have the same score, the one with fewer moves wins.

When you have achieved your best score, you can challenge your friends to see if they can beat you.

Start
Here

Climb the
blackberry
bush?
Go to 23

Head for the
orchard?
Go to 3

1

You cautiously edge your way out of your home in the old log. Your ears are tuned to catch the slightest sound, and you sniff the air for the scent of possible danger, your whiskers quivering. You would rather wait until after dark to forage for food; but your stores are empty and you are very hungry. To your right is a blackberry bush with lots of ripe fruit on it, and straight through the woods is an orchard with lots of fallen apples. Perhaps it would be safer to scurry through the undergrowth to your left, keeping under the cover of the leaves. You might find something tasty hiding under the bushes. You hesitate—all sorts of creatures are around you, just waiting to catch a tasty mouse. Which way do you go?

Turn left through the undergrowth? Go to 17

Still terribly hungry, you emerge from the long grass and stop. You can't believe your eyes! Is that a snake or a legless glass lizard slithering across the path? Thank goodness, it's a lizard. Should you attack? Be careful. You have never killed one before, and you might make a lot of noise trying. Noise is something you want to avoid in order to keep safe. Why not take shelter in the pile of logs until the temptation is gone? Or else you could dash up the path to the nearby sheds and look for something to eat. But be careful, there is not much cover up by the sheds. What is your decision?

**Hide in the logs?
Go to 11**

+ 6 Points

Head for the
trees?
Go to 15

Carry some of
the apple into
a burrow?
Go to 22

3

Go into the
beehive?
Go to 13

At the edge of the woods lies the orchard, with crunchy apples everywhere and the smell of honey gently wafting over from a beehive. Suddenly, some bees buzz out of the opening. Does this mean the beehive is occupied by a swarm? Or are they only harmless drones? The honey smells so good that you would almost dare anything. Why not go in? Or you could bite off a chunk of a nearby apple and carry it into a burrow nearby. Or could you take your food up into the nearest tree, in search of a new storage place?

4

Wrong choice! The hawk saw you even from up high. It dived, grabbed you, and carried you off. Go back to 1.

– 4 Points

Expert Tip
The average life expectancy of a mouse in the wild is only a few months. This is probably just as well because a female mouse can have up to thirty-six babies a year, and the young ones are able to mate within a month or so. Gestation, the period of time between conceiving and delivering the babies, is twenty-five to twenty-six days, and the female is able to mate again within a couple of hours after birth. Despite the high death rate of mice and rats, there are more of them than there are people in the world.

5

Fantastic! You guarded your precious stores so bravely that the squirrel gave up in disgust. Go on to 2 in triumph.

+ 10 Points

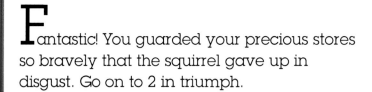

Expert Tip
These mice may have more than one nesting and storage place. They often make nests out of finely shredded grass at the bottom of their burrows, and sometimes they take over birds' nests which are no longer in use. They may use the nest either as a home or as a storage place for food. They sometimes even make a "roof" for the nest out of moss. Mice feel safer underground, and they often have elaborate burrows under the roots of trees where they store nuts, grains, seeds, and berries. They also make extensive tunnels under fallen leaves so that they can travel unseen.

6

Y̶ou make a dash for it and end up in a different part of the tunnel. But you still don't feel safe here. Go on to 15 in search of a better place to store your food.

Expert Tip

The mouse usually spends most of the day inside its burrow, venturing out to search for food only as darkness begins to fall. It is expert at accumulating hordes of berries, nuts, peas, and grains by making constant journeys to the fields and carrying food back in its mouth. Although the mouse does not hibernate in the winter, it does have to store large amounts of food for the lean, cold winter months.

— 9 Points

7

A̶s you clambered onto the rose bush, you lost your footing and fell into the water You couldn't get out and you drowned. Go back to 1.

Expert Tip

These mice can swim for long distances, but they must be able to climb out of the water. On dry land, they are very clean animals who carefully comb dirt out of their fur with their front paws.

+ 3 Points

Collect the scraps and eat under cover? Go to 16

Eat the food where you are and then move on? Go to 23

8

Take a sip
of orange
juice?
Go to 21

The only thought in your mind is escape as you leap through the undergrowth—that is, until you run across the remains of a picnic. What luck! The extremely tempting smell of orange juice is coming from that plastic container over there. Should you try to get your head inside the container to get a drink? You would be well hidden, so you wouldn't have to worry about being seen. Why don't you collect odd scraps of cookies and apples and take them home? Or else you could snatch a quick bite before hurrying away. What will you do?

+ 5 Points

Have a drink?
Go to 7

As you sit on the steps of the shed grooming your coat, you wonder which way to go. All is quiet here, so you are safe. You'd rather be outside, but there is so much food to be found in these gardeners' sheds that they have become one of your favorite places. Why not go inside and see what's there? Or would you like a drink of water? You could climb along the rose bush to the water tub. Or you could chew on that delicious plastic wire before you disappear into the woods again. What shall it be?

Chew on the wire, then go to the woods?
Go to 17

Go inside the shed?
Go to 10

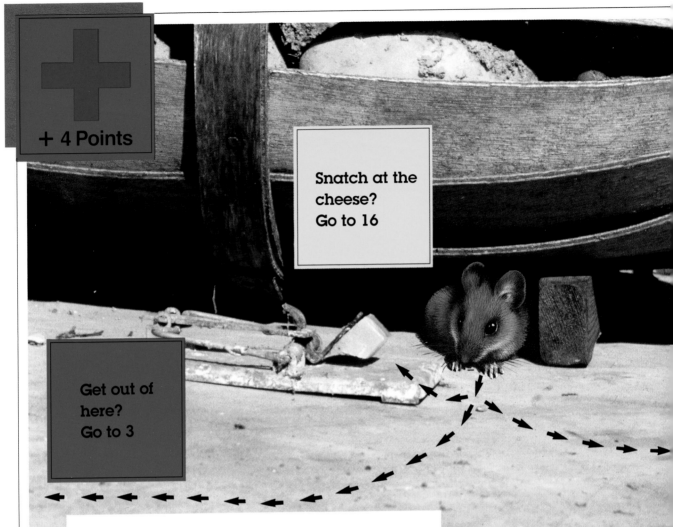

+ 4 Points

Snatch at the cheese?
Go to 16

Get out of here?
Go to 3

What a wonderful collection of smells there are here. Look, there's a tin full of seeds lying on the floor to your left. Or how about investigating the basket of potatoes above you? The thing that is making your nose twitch the most is the mouth-watering smell that all mice love—a bit of cheese! It's in a trap, but you are an old hand at pulling out the cheese before the trap snaps shut. Can you do it once more? You know there is a gardener nearby who might come in at any moment, so you have no time to waste. Perhaps you'd better just get out of here. Quick!

10

Nibble the
seeds on the
tray?
Go to 12

11

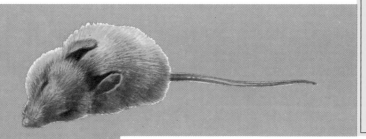

— 10 Points

You didn't look carefully. Behind the log was a rat just waiting for you. He thought you made a tasty lunch. Go back to 1.

Expert Tip
The world is not overrun with mice because rodents are the main food of carnivores, or meat-eating, creatures. Hawks, owls, rats, crows, foxes, snakes, and cats are just some of the many animals that feed on mice.

12

— 7 Points

Unfortunately, you chose the wrong food. The seeds were poisoned; that's why they were bluish in color. Go back to 1 and start again.

Expert Tip
Where humans go, so do mice—and usually uninvited! Gardeners and farmers consider mice to be pests, and some put out poison to destroy them. These poisoned baits are dangerous to birds and other animals who might accidentally eat the poison, as well as to dogs, cats, and owls who catch and eat the poisoned mice. Traps which catch the mice alive are better; the mice can then be released in an area where they will do no harm.

+ 4 Points

Yοu were lucky! The main swarm of bees had left the hive, and it was empty except for the drones, which don't sting. Have a feast on the honey. Go on to 2 when you have had enough to eat.

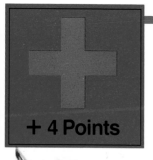

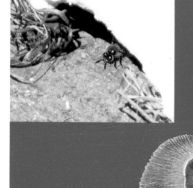

Expert Tip
Mice can only succeed in raiding a beehive if the swarm, or main mass, of bees is absent. The worker bees, if present, will sting. A mouse's favorite foods include: beans, seeds, flower buds, nuts, honey, apples, small birds' eggs, and snails. Mice have long front teeth known as incisors. These teeth are constantly growing, and the mice must gnaw on hard substances, such as nuts, to keep them in good shape. You can sometimes tell what kind of mouse has been feeding on the nuts by the shape of the hole left in the empty shell.

+ 5 Points

It wasn't worth defending your stores against the squirrel. You might have been hurt. It is better to collect more food than to try to protect a few old scraps. Move on to 8.

Expert Tip
Mice survive by relying both on their excellent senses of smell, hearing, and sight, and on their speed and ability to jump. While out in the open, mice usually bound in zigzagging jumps, which make them very difficult to catch. Mice can leap more than three feet into the air or up into the branches of a tree to escape their enemies. They know their territory and do not often roam far from home.

You are delighted with what you have found—a deserted bird's nest, sheltered and hidden from prying eyes. As you drop your mouthful into the nest, you hear a rustling in the leaves behind you. It gets closer and louder, until suddenly, two beady eyes peer out at you from the branches. It is a gray squirrel, and he is always raiding your stores. What do you do? Defend your stores or leap to the ground in search of a better place to hide your food?

15

Defend your
stores?
Go to 5

Leap away
from the
squirrel?
Go to 14

+ 10 Points

At last you are home again in the safety of your nest. You have brought back ample food stores, and you won't need to risk foraging in the daylight for some time to come. Your tummy is full, and your adventures have exhausted you. Sleep well.

Now add up all your SURVIVAL points to get your SURVIVAL score. If you want to improve your score, you can turn back to the beginning and make a new set of choices for a completely different adventure in your life as a mouse.

16

+ 5 Points

You are very excited—you have just spied a juicy caterpillar that has dropped down from a bush overhead and landed on a toadstool. What a tasty meal! But suddenly, with utter horror, your sensitive nose begins to pick up the unmistakable, pungent scent of cat. Is there time to seize the caterpillar before leaping into the bushes to the left? Perhaps you should grab it and dive into the nearby hole. Or would it be better to bound away, hoping to outwit the cat? There is no time to think. Just move.

Snatch the caterpillar and leap into the bushes?
Go to 3

Run away as fast as you can?
Go to 19

Dive into the
hole?
Go to 22

18

W ell done. The other mouse was frightened away by your approach and you got its stores. Go on to 10 for even more food.

Go on to 10 for even more food.

+ 7 Points

Expert Tip
These mice get along well in the open, often sharing a patch where food is abundant. They will, however, occasionally fight during the breeding season. When two strangers meet, they will sometimes stand on their hind legs and either sniff noses or "box" for a moment or two.

19

T hat was a bad move. The cat easily caught up with you and when you tried to hide, it stalked and then killed you instantly. Go back to 1 and start again!

Go back to 1 and start again!

– 12 Points

Expert Tip
These mice are about three and a half inches long, with a tail of about the same length. The long tail helps the mouse to keep its balance. When hiding in the woods, the mouse is very difficult to spot. Its senses of smell and hearing are acute, and its large, bulging eyes give this mouse a wide field of vision. Its long, sensitive whiskers help the mouse to feel its way in the dark and through its tunnels.

+ 8 Points

Y̶ou managed to kill the glass lizard. Normally, you wouldn't try for anything so big, but you were desperate for food and didn't want to be out in the daylight for too long. Go on to 9.

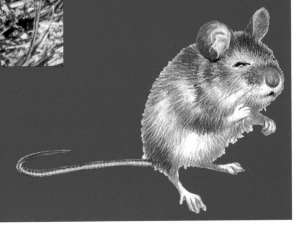

Expert Tip
One of the main differences between a glass lizard and a snake is that the lizard has eyelids and can close its eyes, which no snake can do. The glass lizard's scales are smooth and shiny; and while mice are very fond of eating them, they are not easily caught.

− 10 Points

A̶s you went to investigate the inside of the bottle, your paws slipped. You couldn't grasp the smooth surface of the sides and you were trapped inside. Go back to 1.

Expert Tip
People often leave bottles or plastic containers lying around after a picnic, and these can easily trap small creatures whose curiosity and hunger can lead them inside. Once inside, the creature can neither get a firm foothold on the slippery walls, nor turn around; and it will eventually die.

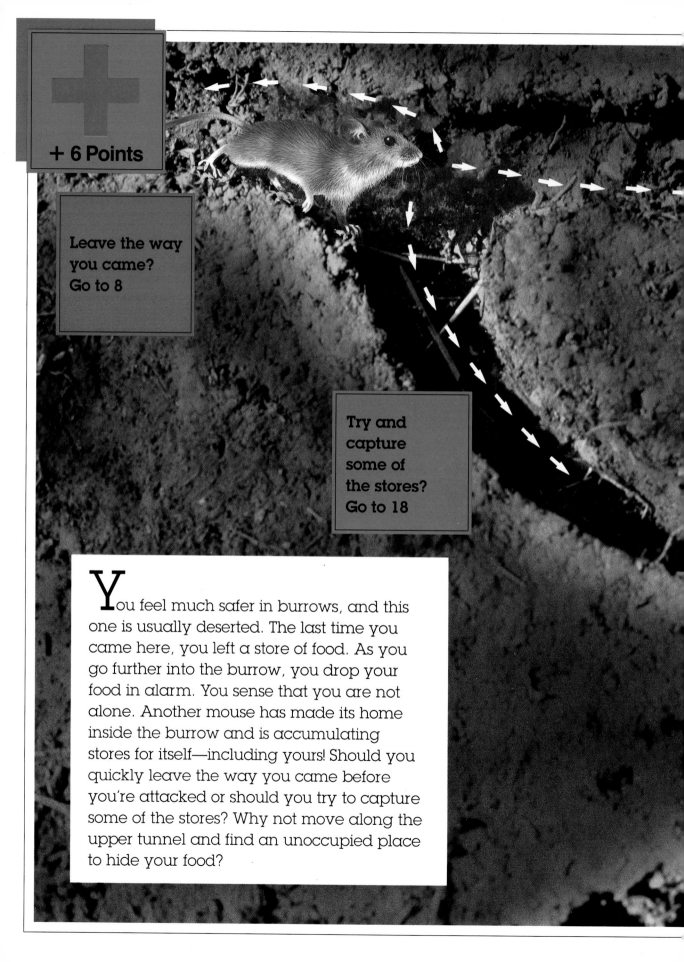

+ 6 Points

Leave the way
you came?
Go to 8

Try and
capture
some of
the stores?
Go to 18

You feel much safer in burrows, and this one is usually deserted. The last time you came here, you left a store of food. As you go further into the burrow, you drop your food in alarm. You sense that you are not alone. Another mouse has made its home inside the burrow and is accumulating stores for itself—including yours! Should you quickly leave the way you came before you're attacked or should you try to capture some of the stores? Why not move along the upper tunnel and find an unoccupied place to hide your food?

Move along
the upper
tunnel?
Go to 6

+ 6 Points

Carry a berry
into the
woods?
Go to 17